Heart healing after breakup
by Marion Baldwin

First published 2021

Publishing partner: Paragon Publishing, Rothersthorpe

ISBN 978-1-78222-848-6

Book design, layout and production management by Into Print
www.intoprint.net
01604 832149

TABLE OF CONTENTS

ABOUT THE AUTHOR

Marion is an inspiring natural healer and professional course leader. She has spent many years researching and experiencing natural healing methods. She is an enthusiastic ambassador for the happiness and healing changes they can bring to your life.

This workbook (and course) is the result of her own healing journey after a particularly upsetting breakup a few years ago. After using the techniques in this workbook, she has now found peace, happiness and love. While difficult at the time, she now feels that the healing journey she experienced has resulted in more love and happiness in her life.

This workbook accompanies the 'Heart Healing after Breakup' course. However, it also stands alone as a guide for those who would like more privacy following a relationship breakup and prefer one to one support rather than being part of a group.

This is one of several courses Marion has developed. She would love to welcome you onto her courses so that you too can learn about the benefits of these wonderful healing methods.

More details can be found at www.spiritedwoman.co.uk

INTRODUCTION

This workbook is about how to navigate the journey from heartache to happiness after the breakup of a relationship.

You have chosen it for a reason. Right now, your heart may be hurting, you feel unhappy and life may look grey. Know that one day you will feel better than you do today, and that you are NOT alone in this.

It is part of being human to experience loss and grief, it does have a place on the wheel of life, but so does healing, joy, peace and love.

I hope that this book will encourage you along your journey, offering comfort, solace and a route to your own inner wisdom and healing. Then, when the time is right, you will find yourself back on the road to love and happiness again.

I invite you to read on . . . .

ABOUT THIS BOOK

The written word is a linear process, but the healing journey is not. It leads you the way of your own inner wisdom. It's more meandering, as shown on the roadmap. It is certainly not a straight road.

There is no right or wrong way to go. This is your unique journey and however it is done is entirely right for you. Choose which part of the workbook feels right at any given time. You may come back to the same section many times, or start at the middle or end, or leave some of it out altogether. Its entirely up to you.

As a linear book, it is divided into sections, each section representing a well-documented stage on the healing journey. You may experience some or all of these stages, as well as other stages unique to you.

At the end of each section there is a summary of 'The Healing Companions' recommended for that particular part of the journey. These include natural remedies, inspiring reading, music and meditation. You will find more details about 'The Healing Companions' and how to use them next.

When going through a breakup you can often feel tender and confused, with your mind in turmoil. In view of this, I have created the workbook in an 'easy to read' style with clear words and few technical terms.

'The spiritual (healing) journey is individual and highly personal. It can't be organised or regulated. It isn't true that everyone should follow one path. Listen to your own truth'

Ram Dass - American spiritual teacher, psychologist and author of 'Be Here Now'.

THE HEALING COMPANIONS

These are the things I have found enormously helpful on my own healing journey, I hope you will find some of them supportive on your journey. If they are unfamiliar to you, I would suggest you try them with an open mind and heart. You will soon know if they are for you or not, and that is fine. Trying new things will bring you closer to finding what works for you. Trust your own instincts and feelings.

Note that some of the remedies appear often as they are multifunctional and beneficial for many stages of this journey.

Physical	These are suggestions to comfort and nurture your body and soul in the early stages of this journey. As you move on there are suggestions to energise, bring confidence, indulge and beautify as your journey progresses.
Music	Music has the capacity to change or enhance your mood. It doesn't matter what song or piece of music you listen to, just choose one you like. It's personal.
	Initially you may choose sad music which can encourage tears and letting go. As the journey progresses you might want to listen to uplifting music or comforting sounds or do some joyful dancing. Use music to accompany your many feelings on this journey. It will help you feel better. Look up 'Inspiring music' on YouTube.
Inspiring Reading	There is so much solace and wisdom to be found in books, articles and postings online. Your intuition will guide you to the things that are right for you. Sometimes you'll come across a book or words that provide just what you need in the present moment - you might call it 'serendipity' - a seeming gift or finding something good accidentally.
	Look up these inspirational authors - Louise L Hay, Dr Wayne Dyer, Kahlil Gibran, Eckhart Tolle, Dalai Lama ...
	Check out www.livehappy.com

Meditation	The physical and emotional benefits of Meditation are many - stress, anxiety and depression diminish as you feel more peaceful. Meditation can be done anywhere. You don't need a special chair, clothing or place. However, it can be helpful to meditate each day at the same time. You can start with just a few minutes, moving up to whatever time you like. How to ... Meditate 1. Sit somewhere quiet and comfortable where you are not going to be disturbed. 2. Close your eyes and focus your attention on the in-and-out breath of your own body. 3. As you do this, its normal to get distracted by your own thoughts. As soon as you notice that your mind has wandered, gently return your attention back to your breath without any self-judgement. As you practice this, you will find a place of quiet and peace within and will start to feel calmer as you navigate this journey. You may also find that solutions to the issues you are experiencing come into you mind, either during meditation or afterwards. If you are new to this, you can find guided meditations online which will show you the way. www.mindful.org/how-to-meditate/
Affirmation	Affirmations are sayings or helpful words that you think, read, and/or write down. They imprint into your subconscious and can change the way you feel. They are immensely helpful in moving your minds attention from repetitive negative thoughts into a more positive place. It's a loving action you can do for yourself.

Affirmation (continued)	In fact, we always have 'affirmations' going through our minds, but there are many benefits when we direct our thoughts in a more conscious and positive way.

'Every word you speak, or think is an affirmation the subconscious is always listening' -

Louise L Hay was an American motivational author and the founder of Hay House, author of 'You can Heal your Life'.

How to use ... Affirmations

Pick one or two affirmations, you can make them up yourself, or find them online or in books by Louise L Hay and others. Write them in a journal or on post-it notes and place them where you can read them often.

Regularly repeat them in your mind and/or say them out loud in your car or when alone. Do this with your heart and mind open and receptive. In time you will notice their beneficial effect on your thinking.

Affirmations also work well in conjunction with Havening Touch Technique (details on page 12). When you couple a physical action with a mental thought process, the positive messages to the brain are reinforced.

www.louisehay.com/affirmations/

www.havening.org |
| Essential Oils | Essential oils have been used therapeutically for centuries. They are the potent essence of plants, trees and flowers with remarkable healing properties for body, mind and spirit. Their molecules are very fine and are quickly assimilated into the body through the senses. |

Essential Oils (continued)	There are a wide range of oils available to heal and support the physical and emotional states we experience as human beings. They bring many comforts including self-love, clarity, focus, joy, peace, can lift your spirits, ease sore muscles, heal headaches and much more as well as having a beautiful aroma.

How to use ... Essential Oils

Essential oils can be enjoyed in many different ways; however, they are very potent and powerful and should always be used with care and understanding.

As a general rule do not put the concentrated essence directly onto your skin, mix with a carrier oil (a neutral organic oil like sweet almond oil, fractionated coconut oil or argan oil) at a ratio of less than 5% concentrated essential oil to carrier oil.

Always do a patch test on your wrist or arm before using any new oil or blend. Wait for 24 hours and if there is any adverse reaction DO NOT USE.

Different ways to enjoy Essential Oils

Inhale directly from the bottle or add a few drops of diluted oil to cupped hands and inhale deeply.

Add a few drops of oil to:
• a neutral body lotion and massage into your body
• sprinkle on your cltothing, scarves, tissues or jewellery and enjoy the aroma as you go about your day
• add a few drops onto your pillow at night to help you relax and sleep
• splash a few drops into your bath and inhale the aroma in the steam as you bathe
• add a few drops to a room diffuser and experience the lovely aroma in a room

Essential Oils (continued)	You can also find diffusers, candles, room sprays and many other forms of essential oil products in holistic and health shops as well as online.

Do buy organic therapeutic grade oils where possible as they are pure, more potent and effective.

Some of my favourite suppliers are:

www.tisserand.com/essential-oils

www.quinessence.com

www.nealsyardremedies.com

www.doterra.com/GB/en_GB

NOTE: If you are pregnant or suffer from skin allergies or sensitivity, DO NOT USE essential oils without first seeking expert advice. |
| **NOTE:** | If you would like to learn more about Essential Oils, I would love to welcome you onto my 'Wonderful Essential Oils' course.

I also intuitively create a unique blend of oils personalised for you. This will support you in navigating your current challenges with grace and fortitude, bringing comfort and hope.

More details can be found on my website www.spiritedwoman.co.uk. |
| **Natural Remedies & Essences** | Plant and Flower Remedies are an energetic medicine made from the imprint of the living plant's vibrations in water. They have been developed by devoted and gifted therapists over many years.

These remedies are immensely helpful and can assist in bringing comfort, changing your perspective and moving you forward. There are remedies for just about every emotional feeling or situation.

They are like essential oils but are preserved in spring water and taken by mouth. |

Natural Remedies & Essences (continued)	Remedies, like those from Dr Bach, can be found online and in high street shops and health stores. There are guides to help you choose the right remedy to assist with how you are feeling. Also experienced plant and flower therapists can create a unique remedy for you. How to use ... Plant and Flower Remedies Put a few drops, usually 3 to start, under your tongue at regular intervals during the day or, add a few drops to a glass of spring water to sip during the day. The effect is subtle and can take a few days to become apparent, but be patient, the remedies are highly effective in moving you into a different mind-set. www.bachflower.com/original-bach-flower-remedies www.rosetodd.com/bach-flower-essences
Crystals	Crystals have formed over millennia absorbing the electromagnetic energy of the earth. The energy of crystals can be transmitted and absorbed by the body for healing and promoting health, well-being and inner peace. Scientific research has been conducted on how crystals resonate and heal the body. More details about this are at: www.healyourlife.com/how-crystals-work-the-science-of-crystal-healing There are a wide range of crystals which heal and support the physical and emotional states we experience as human beings. They bring many comforts including emotional balance, chakra healing and are beautiful to work with.

Crystals (continued)	How to use ... Crystals

Crystals can be:

• kept with you in a pocket and held or rubbed when you feel in need of comfort or support
• worn on the body in jewellery as pendants, bracelets or earrings
• put under your pillow as you sleep
• placed on the relevant body chakras when in meditation or resting.

Judy Hall is the pioneer of Crystal Healing. More information can be found at: www.judyhall.co.uk

Crystals also work well in conjunction with Essential Oils. A few drops of a complimentary oil can be added to a crystal to increase its effectiveness. For example, a drop of rose oil on rose quartz works beautifully. |
| Havening Touch | Havening Touch Technique is a self-healing method using four simple exercises that can be done anywhere. The exercises are very comforting bringing healing to the mind, body and spirit at a deep level. Over time, regular use can bring healing and peace to negative emotional or traumatic experiences, reducing anxiety and depression.

The method is backed up by scientific research which shows beneficial changes to the brain when practiced regularly. It works by disrupting the link between the memory of a traumatic event from the distress it continues to cause, and can bring resolution, peace and a happier life.

Havening Touch Technique is extremely helpful in shifting the emotional trauma experienced after a break up and preventing it from adversely affecting future relationships. |

Havening Touch (continued)	Havening Touch Technique also works well in conjunction with Affirmations. When you couple a physical action with a mental thought process the positive messages to the brain are reinforced.
	There are Havening Touch therapists who are experienced with this method of healing.
	You can find more details online at www.havening.org
	Also search on YouTube for 'Facilitated Self Havening with Dr Robin Youngson' a soothing guided meditation using this healing model.
Reiki	Reiki is spiritually guided healing, using universal life force energy. It is a simple, natural and safe method of healing everyone can learn and use. It is effective in ameliorating many physical and emotional conditions.
	You can find Reiki courses and therapists online
	www.reiki.org.uk
	www.healing-reiki.org.uk
EFT Emotional Freedom Technique (Tapping)	EFT is a process to assist with resolving emotional issues by tapping with your fingertips on acupressure points on the body. This works to release blockages in the energy system which are the source of emotional distress and discomfort.
	It is a practical and simple process that can be done anywhere and restores trust and confidence in our own natural healing abilities. There are no drugs, no equipment is needed, and this technique can give immediate release from emotional distress.
	You can find EFT therapists online, and get more information at:
	www.thetappingsolution.com www.london-eft.org.uk

Healing Counselling and Standard Medicine	There are many forms of healing, counselling and therapy available with kind and supportive therapists. Your medical doctor can also assist with counselling and/or medication if you wish to compliment the above with a more conventional approach.

NOTE: I have used all the 'Healing Companions' over many years and found them enormously beneficial and comforting. However, this is my personal view and experience. Although I have been practicing many years now, I am not a medical doctor. If you feel unsure, have any skin sensitivities or feel in crisis, I recommend you seek the advice of a registered practitioner, counsellor or medical doctor.

The Roadmap

SHOCK PAIN

ACCEPTANCE

RELEASING

FORGIVENESS

Vale of Tears

FEELING BLUE

LONELINESS

CONTENTMENT

PEACE

HAPPINESS

JOY

LOOKING FORWARD

STAGES OF THE JOURNEY

1. WHAT A SHOCK

2. FEELING BLUE

3. RELEASING (PAIN, REGRET, ANGER)

4. ACCEPTANCE

5. FORGIVENESS (TOUGH ONE!)

6. LONELINESS

7. LOOKING FORWARD

WHAT A SHOCK

WHAT A SHOCK!

If your relationship is over, even if you have felt the end coming, there is always shock, distress and a space in your life that your ex used to inhabit. These feelings of loss and sadness are not easy and can feel uncomfortable. You may feel confused, your heart may be racing, feel nauseous, or have headaches and/or sleeplessness. All of this is part of the normal process of the mind trying to make sense of a difficult situation. Remember, you will not always feel like this. Be kind and nurturing to yourself, comfort your mind and body until it can process and understand what has happened in its own time.

Denial can be one of the first things you feel with things going through your mind like 'How can this be true', 'Maybe we're not really breaking up'. It is reassuring to know that denial is also a part of loss and grief. It assists us to pace our feelings and is nature's way of letting in only as much as our mind can process at the time.

You may find yourself bargaining in your mind with what you perceive as God/Goddess/Divine Grace, bringing thoughts like 'If my lover will come back to me I will never lose my temper again'. You want life to return to what it was and go back in time. Bargaining is a recognised stage on this journey as well. These feelings come up usually for a short time, but they do belong to the past, and you are finding your way forward to a new future. These are just thoughts, they come and go, try not to hold onto them.

Alternatively, you might find that while you initiated the break up you are surprised at your feelings of regret and grief once it's happened. This again is part of the normal process of letting go of the past.

At this time, I would strongly recommend that you refrain from calling or texting your ex, or from following them on social media. Keeping in touch like this, when you have broken up, only sets you back, fostering false hopes, preventing wounds from healing and hurting your feelings again. Even if you are hoping for reconciliation, no contact is still advisable as it gives your ex space to think about life without you.

If you must be in touch with your ex for any reason, keep it business-like and brief. Take control and use a medium that is the easiest for you, for example email. You can then decide to deal with any replies at a time that works well for you and when you feel strong enough to face the task.

Nurture yourself during this stage, find one of the healing companions to assist you, be kind to yourself. This is a time for you to take care of yourself with deeply comforting and nurturing actions and thoughts.

It is good to recognise that the depth of your distress and unhappiness is a measure of the depth of love you are capable of feeling. This capacity to love can be used to comfort yourself. If you find this a difficult concept - imagine how you would feel if a good friend of yours was in the same situation you are in now. You would feel love and compassion for them and want to help them in any way you could. Turn this love and compassion towards yourself, befriend yourself, recognise the loving person you are who is feeling hurt at the moment.

'Let go of people who aren't ready to love you yet. This is the hardest thing you'll have to do in your life, and it will also be the most important. Stop giving your love to those who aren't ready to love you yet'

- Sir Anthony Hopkins - Actor

HEALING COMPANIONS – WHAT A SHOCK!

Physical	Soft and comforting clothes and bedding. Hot baths with candles, hot chocolate, nice food, forget about the diet for now.
	You might not feel like this but a walk in nature is very restorative.
	You might like to consider a 'Break Up' Retreat.
Music	Remember music can positively change your mood. Play music you love, if you feel like crying put on something sad and let the tears flow and go. (The slow movement of Bach's Double Violin concerto, Mozart's Clarinet Concerto, Adele, Ed Sheeran, Andrea Bocelli)
	If you feel angry punch out the air to Tchaikovsky's 1812. If you want to be uplifted put on some loud music and dance or listen to Bob Marley.
Inspiring Reading	'You can Heal your Heart' - Louise L Hay & David Kessler
	'Change your Thoughts, Change your Life' - Dr Wayne Dyer
Meditate	When you feel shocked, it can be difficult to meditate. Look on YouTube for guided meditations for shock and relax into one.
	www.mindful.org/how-to-meditate/
Affirm	*'I may not understand why my relationship has ended, but I accept this as reality so my healing can begin' *'My past relationship is completed; I accept the healing and the lessons learned'
	'All is well in my world' - Louise L Hay

Affirm (continued)	'Even though I feel shocked and distressed there is love in my life' – Louise L Hay *From 'You can Heal your Heart' - by Louise L Hay & David Kessler
	NOTE: Affirmations also work well in conjunction with Havening Touch Technique. When you couple a physical action with a mental thought process, the positive messages to the brain are reinforced.
Essential Oils	Rose - is deeply nurturing, comforting and supports letting go of barriers around the heart Basil - alleviates the effects of shock when under mental strain Peppermint - brings joy and buoyancy during times of emotional unhappiness Geranium - helps heal a broken heart Wild Orange - supports a positive mood and is joyful and uplifting Ready mixed blends: 'Console' or 'Forgive' from DoTerra 'Calming' or 'Women's Balance' from Neal's Yard www.tisserand.com/essential-oils www.quinessence.com www.nealsyardremedies.com www.doterra.com/GB/en_GB

Natural Remedies and Essences	Bleeding Heart Flower Essence - to heal the heart www.powerfloweressences.com BACH FLOWER REMEDIES Rescue Remedy - for shock White Chestnut - for incessant thoughts, overthinking Sweet Chestnut - for feelings of desolation Honeysuckle - for when you are living in your memories and not present in the world. www.bachflower.com/original-bach-flower-remedies www.rosetodd.com/bach-flower-essences/
Crystals	Rose Quartz - is the master emotional healer Smoky Quartz - stabilises emotions when in crisis Amethyst - balances emotional highs and lows For more information go to www.judyhall.co.uk
Havening Touch	If you are attracted to this self-healing method you can find more details online at havening.org NOTE: Havening Touch Technique also works well in conjunction with Affirmations. When you couple a physical action with a mental thought process the positive messages to the brain are reinforced.
Reiki	If you are attracted to this healing model, look for Reiki courses and therapists online. www.reiki.org.uk www.healing-reiki.org.uk

EFT Emotional Freedom Technique	If you are attracted to this healing model you can find more details at: www.thetappingsolution.com
Healing Counselling and Standard Medicine	There are many forms of healing, counselling and therapy available with kind and supportive therapists. Your medical doctor can also assist with counselling and/or medication if you wish to compliment the above with a more conventional approach.

NOTES

FEELING BLUE - DEPRESSION

FEELING BLUE - DEPRESSION

Loss in your life can trigger deep sadness and sometimes depression. This response is normal and appropriate to the real loss of a meaningful relationship. In fact, it would be more unusual not to experience these feelings.

No-one wants to find themselves here in this unhappy place, feeling overwhelmed and emotionally exhausted. Know that you are not alone and that these feelings will not last forever.

You may feel the need to keep busy. This is one way of alleviating the distress for a short time. But what happens as soon as you stop busying, or try to sleep, the emotions come flooding in. These feelings have to find their way out and be faced at some point. You don't have to do this alone and you do have choice in how and when you deal with them. Find a way that feels easiest for you, confide in a good friend and/or consider joining a group where you will meet others going through a similar process.

Alternatively, you may want to withdraw from life, this too can be healing for a short period. However, you need to make sure that you do not isolate yourself for too long. If you are on your own too much or finding it difficult to move out of this stage, reach out to good friends, find a counsellor or visit your doctor.

Above all, be kind and nurture yourself through this time.

HEALING COMPANIONS – FEELING BLUE

Physical	Talk to a good friend, counsellor or your doctor.
	Walk in nature, by a river or flowing water, or in a wood or across fields. Breathe in the fresh air, look around and remember how nature recovers after the fallowness of the winter. You can too.
Music	Remember music can positively change your mood. Play music you find comforting, Mozart or Schubert. Look up soothing sounds on Spotify.
	To be uplifted - play 'Here comes the Sun' by the Beatles or 'Be Happy' by Bob Marley
	Google 'The most uplifting songs ever'
Inspiring	'The Road Less Travelled' – Dr F Scott Peck
	'Living an Inspired Life' – Dr Wayne Dyer
	'Only people who are capable of loving strongly can also suffer great sorrow, but this same capacity of loving serves to counteract their grief and heals them'. Leo Tolstoy
Meditate	Meditation can be very comforting and helpful, but when you feel depressed and unhappy it can be difficult to do. Look online for some guided meditations and allow yourself to relax into them.
	Google 'Meditation for Depression & Sadness: Guided Mindfulness Meditation'
	www.mindful.org/how-to-meditate/

Affirm	'I feel my grief, but am not going to wallow in unhappy feelings' - Louise L Hay 'I feel my grief and accept it as a mark of my humanity and capacity to love' - Louise L Hay 'Healing takes time and I give myself this gift' – 'Grief Loss & Mourning Affirmations' online. NOTE: Affirmations also work well in conjunction with Havening Touch Technique. When you couple a physical action with a mental thought process, the positive messages to the brain are reinforced.
Essential Oils	Rose - deeply nurturing and comforting, supports letting go of barriers around the heart Wild Orange - uplifting and joyful Lemongrass - dispels feelings of despair and assists in entering a healing mode. Ready mixed blends: 'Hope' and 'In Tune' from DoTerra 'Optimism' from Neal's Yard www.tisserand.com/essential-oils www.quinessence.com www.neilsyardremedies.com www.doterra.com/GB/en_GB

Natural Remedies Natural & Essences	Mustard Flower Essence – to alleviate grief www.powerfloweressences.com BACH FLOWER REMEDIES Star of Bethlehem - for consolation and comfort in grief Gorse - for when you feel hopeless Hornbeam - for when you feel weary and find it difficult to cope www.bachflower.com/symptoms-of-depression www.rosetodd.com/bach-flower-essences/
Crystals	Labradorite – to alleviate the symptoms of reactive depression – (depression as a reaction to events that have happened) Blue Lace Agate – to bring release from situations where you feel rejected Amethyst – to dispel fear and anxiety, ease sadness and grief and helps you to adjust to loss.
Havening Touch	If you are attracted to this self-healing method you can find more details online and at havening.org NOTE: Havening Touch Technique also works well in conjunction with Affirmations. When you couple a physical action with a mental thought process the positive messages to the brain are reinforced.

Reiki	If you are attracted to this healing model, look for Reiki courses and therapists online. www.reiki.org.uk www.healing-reiki.org.uk
EFT Emotional Freedom Technique	If you are attracted to this healing model you can find more details at www.thetappingsolution.com
Healing Counselling and Standard Medicine	There are many forms of healing, counselling and therapy available with kind and supportive therapists. Your medical doctor can also assist with counselling and/or medication if you wish to compliment the above with a more conventional approach. NOTE: Be aware of how you are feeling, if you feel suicidal, can't get out of bed or can't seem to move on from your loss, seek the assistance of a counsellor who specialises in grief and loss.

RELEASING ANGER AND PAIN

RELEASING ANGER AND PAIN

Anger is a necessary stage of the healing process. It is a natural human emotion that can help you know when a situation needs to change, show you that you have been hurt, or when your feelings have been ignored or disrespected.

Be willing to feel your anger, even though it is not a comfortable feeling. If you feel angry, it indicates that you have moved on from the depression stage where anger can be suppressed. However, it is very important that you find a way to release your angry feelings. Holding onto anger and taking it into your body has been linked to many health risks including high blood pressure, depression and sleep disturbance.

When we are hurting, it often feels like someone has done something to us. It can be helpful to look at this a different way. Consider that the other person is acting from a closed heart and their behaviour towards you could now cause your heart to close. The challenge is to keep your heart open to the love and healing that is available to you so that your heart is able to love again.

Try to see that you cannot change other people, but you can change yourself and how you are feeling. You can call help from many sources seen and unseen - the healing companions, friends, books, Angels, Divine Grace. As you release the pain and anger you are holding in your body, peace will arrive, and the pain will start to subside.

Remember the sky is always blue and sunny, but sometimes dark clouds stop us seeing the sun and sky. We know the clouds are temporary, but the sky is permanent.

'Holding on to anger is like grasping a hot coal with the intent of throwing it at someone else; you are the one getting burned'

- Dalai Lama - spiritual leader of Tibet

HEALING COMPANIONS - RELEASING ANGER & PAIN

Physical	Vigorous exercise, run, swim, kick a ball, punch a pillow, shout, scream, dance wildly to loud music Throw plates against a wall (safely!!)
Music	Indigenous drums or loud music can release anger. Once released calming meditative music can help to restore your equilibrium.
Inspiring Reading / Writing	Write down all your thoughts, burn the paper (safely) and give these feelings to the wind. Dalai Lama 'Healing Anger' Marianne Williamson 'Return to Love'
Meditation	Meditation can be difficult when you feel angry, but it can be enormously helpful. Search YouTube for 'Guided Meditations to release anger' www.mindful.org/how-to-meditate
Affirm	'I release all my righteous anger' - '111 Powerful Affirmations for Anger' - Alan Young 'I am responsible for my own Happiness' - Louise L Hay 'With every breath I take I am sending love, gratitude and healing to every single cell in my body'* *www.healing-affirmations.com/release-transform-anger NOTE: Affirmations also work well in conjunction with Havening Touch Technique. When you couple a physical mental thought process, the positive messages to the brain are reinforced.

Essential Oils	Thyme - releases trapped feelings of anger and frustration
	Cardamom – brings balance and clarity when angry and frustrated
	Geranium – softens anger and heals emotional wounds
	Ylang Ylang - the ultimate healer of past hurts, releases sadness, anger and emotional trauma, connects the mind and heart and brings joyful feelings back.
	Wild Orange – uplifting and joyful
	Ready mixed blends: 'HD Clear' or 'Air' from DoTerra
	'De-Stress' from Neal's Yard
	www.tisserand.com/essential-oils
	www.quinessence.com
	www.nealsyardremedies.com
	www.doterra.com/GB/en_GB
Natural Remedies & Essences	Scarlet Monkeyflower - a transformative remedy that addresses the fears associated with anger issues
	www.powerfloweressences.com
	Chamomile - Calming agent that brings emotional balance and helps diffuse feelings of anger.
	www.aquariusflowerremedies.com
	BACH FLOWER REMEDIES
	Rescue Remedy - for shock and fear
	Holly - for release of Anger
	Impatiens - for patience
	www.bachflower.com/original-bach-flower-remedies www.rosetodd.com/bach-flower-essences/

Crystals	Blue Lace Agate - dissolves anger replacing it with peace

Green Aventurine - calms anger and promotes well being

Carnelian - calms anger

Bloodstone - reduces all forms of anger |
| Havening Touch | If you are attracted to this self-healing method you can find more details online and at www.havening.org

NOTE: Havening Touch Technique also works well in conjunction with Affirmations. When you couple a physical action with a mental thought process the positive messages to the brain are reinforced. |
| Reiki | If you are attracted to this healing model, look for Reiki courses and therapists online.

www.reiki.org.uk

www.healing-reiki.org.uk |
| EFT Emotional Freedom Technique | If you are attracted to this healing model you can find more details at

www.thetappingsolution.com |
| Healing | There are many forms of healing, counselling and therapy available with kind and supportive therapists.

Your medical doctor can also assist with counselling and/or medication if you wish to compliment the above with a more conventional approach. |

NOTES

ACCEPTANCE

ACCEPTANCE

Acceptance is often thought of as being 'all right' or 'OK' with what has happened. While you may not feel this, starting to accept the reality of what has happened is an indication that you are in a good place on your healing journey.

It can still be difficult, you can't replace what has been lost and you may still have regrets, unhappy feelings and look at the past as 'rose tinted'. This does not make you a victim, it makes you a human being in pain, processing the normal feelings of grief and the loss of a hoped-for future.

The feelings are horrible, there is no other way to say it. But they can be released. You can find happiness again once you truly accept and release the past. There will be bad days and good days, with the good increasing with time.

Use the 'Healing Companions' to nurture yourself through this stage. Start to reach out, make new connections, invest in your friendships and in a loving relationship with yourself.

HEALING COMPANIONS - ACCEPTANCE

Physical	Gardening, walking in nature, swimming. Change your environment, move the furniture around, get some new pictures, decorate. Start a new exercise class or an art class at your local college.
Music	Positive uplifting music, or if you feel like looking inwards - eastern meditation music. There are lots of options online.
Inspired Reading	'You can Heal your Life' – Louise L Hay 'Happiness is the Way' – Dr Wayne Dyer 'Serenity Prayer' – Reinhold Niebuhr *'God/Goddess/Universal Grace - grant me the SERENITY to accept the things I cannot change, the COURAGE to change the things I can and the WISDOM to know the difference'* *'When we can no longer change a situation, we are challenged to change ourselves'* - Victor Frankl
Meditation	Look online for guided meditations for acceptance. www.mindful.org/how-to-meditate/
Affirm	'Even though I don't understand why we split up, I accept this as reality so that healing can begin'* 'Relationships will come and go; I am always here for myself'* 'The past is over; I look forward to the future with hope in my heart'* 'I totally release all past experiences, I am free'*

Affirm (continued)	*'You can Heal your Heart' - by Louise L Hay & David Kessler NOTE: Affirmations also work well in conjunction with Havening Touch Technique. When you couple a physical action with a mental thought process, the positive messages to the brain are reinforced.
Essential Oils	Rose - is deeply nurturing and comforting Spikenard - helps to accept life how it IS and brings peace Bergamot - supports self-acceptance and self-love, brings optimism and hope Ylang Ylang - the ultimate healer of past hurts, releases sadness, anger and emotional trauma, connects the mind and heart and brings joyful feelings back. Rosemary - is supportive at times of transition and change Ready mixed blends: 'Acceptance' blend for transition and adapting to new changes. 'Peace and Calming' - is powerful when used with Acceptance blend. www.experience-essential-oils.com 'Hope' from DoTerra; 'Calming' from Neal's Yard www.tisserand.com/essential-oils www.quinessence.com www.nealsyardremedies.com www.doterra.com/GB/en_GB

Natural Remedies & Essences	**BACH FLOWER REMEDIES** Walnut – for change and protection from outside influences. www.bachflower.com/original-bach-flower-remedies www.rosetodd.com/bach-flower-essences/ 'Acceptance Essence' – gentle calming and balancing essence that helps with acceptance of situation as it is and keeps you on an even keel. www.ausspiritessences.com.au
Crystals	Crysocolla - gives courage to deal with the current situation. Amethyst - alleviates sadness and grief and helps accept and adjust to loss Sodalite - brings emotional clarity Jet - reduces the hold of fear and sadness Malachite - balances emotions, reduces stress and increases hope. Rose Quartz - is comforting and supporting
Havening Touch	If you are attracted to this self-healing method you can find more details online and at www.havening.org NOTE: Havening Touch Technique also works well in conjunction with Affirmations. When you couple a physical action with a mental thought process the positive messages to the brain are reinforced.
Reiki	If you are attracted to this healing model, look for Reiki courses and therapists online. www.reiki.org.uk www.healing-reiki.org.uk

Healing Counselling & Standard Medicine	There are many forms of healing, counselling and therapy available with kind and supportive therapists. Your medical doctor can also assist with counselling and/or medication if you wish to compliment the above with a more conventional approach.
	'Peace is the result of retraining your mind to process life as it is, rather than as you think it should be' Dr Wayne Dyer was an American self-help and spiritual author and a motivational speaker.

FORGIVENESS

FORGIVENESS

Forgiving someone is not easy, but so necessary.

It's important to understand that forgiveness is not about releasing the person who hurt or wronged you from their guilt, that is for them to work out for themselves. It's an act of self-love for you, challenging you to let go of negative feelings so that you can feel joy, peace and love again.

Releasing negative feelings and choosing forgiveness of others and yourself, has significant health benefits for mind, body and spirit. It is well documented that holding onto negative feelings causes stress, pain and unhappiness leading to a lack of trust about the future. Being at peace with your feelings brings calm, hope, joy and trust back into your life.

It can be helpful to understand that people are only capable of loving another person in the way they are able to love themselves. If you expect them to act differently, or love as you do, it will only make it more difficult for you. They probably didn't set out to hurt you but are unable or unwilling to behave differently. Really understanding this can take some time, but accepting it is so helpful in moving forward peacefully in your own life.

Remember also to forgive yourself for choices you might wish you'd made differently - for getting yourself into a situation that caused you pain, for not protecting your heart. You did your best, and in most cases acted from love, loving too much, fear of being alone, just being human.

Also remember forgiveness is a courageous thing to do and an attribute of the strong, of the true loving human being - Jesus, Gandhi, Nelson Mandela, Maya Angelou, Martin Luther King and the (extra)-ordinary people who find forgiveness for the perpetrators of awful things against their loved ones.

'Forgiving is a gift to yourself. It frees you from past experiences and relationships. It allows you to live in present time. When you forgive others, you are indeed free' - Louise L Hay

HEALING COMPANIONS - FORGIVENESS

Physical	Walking in nature, hot bath with aromatic oils, massage, comforting clothes and activities. Meeting up with close friends.
Music	'Let it be' - The Beatles - the words are really helpful Eastern meditative music is comforting.
Inspired Reading	Marianne Williamson 'Return to Love' Search online for Dr Wayne Dyer on 'Forgiveness' and '7-lessons-from-famous-people-about forgiving-others'
Affirm	'I forgive, not because they deserve it, but because I deserve peace' - Hala Yasmine Khaled - Thought Catalog 'I move through forgiveness to love' - Louise L Hay 'I forgive myself for not being perfect' - Louise L Hay 'My past relationship is completed; I accept the healing and the lessons learnt' - Louise L Hay 'I love myself; I forgive myself; I totally release all past experiences - I am FREE' - Louise L Hay (Question: Is it better to be right or happy? Choose to be happy) NOTE: Affirmations also work well in conjunction with Havening Touch Technique. When you couple a physical action with a mental thought process, the positive messages to the brain are reinforced.

Meditation	Forgiveness can be difficult, guided meditations on forgiveness can help move on from your feelings of hurt. Look online for these. Google 'Guided meditations for Forgiveness' www.mindful.org/how-to-meditate/ Look up the Hawaiian Ho'oponopono Prayer for forgiveness, it is immensely powerful and healing.
Essential Oils	Geranium - 'The Emotional Healer' - encourages forgiveness and assists in finding trust in yourself and others. Thyme - transforms hate and anger into love and forgiveness Siberian Fir - eases difficult situations, promotes forgiveness. Oil Blends: 'Forgive' Do Terra www.tisserand.com/essential-oils www.quinessence.com www.nealsyardremedies.com www.doterra.com/GB/en_GB
Natural Remedies & Essences	BACH FLOWER REMEDIES Honeysuckle - for letting go of regret and learning to live in the present. www.bachflower.com/original-bach-flower-remedies

	www.rosetodd.com/bach-flower-essences/ Powerflower Essences 'Letting go of the past' essence www.powerfloweressences.com/ forgiveness www.findhornessences.com/forgiveness
Crystals	Rose Quartz - stone of unconditional love brings deep forgiveness and instils peaceful feelings. Green Aventurine - brings compassion and empathy and assists in forgiving others
Havening Touch	If you are attracted to this self-healing method you can find more details online and at www.havening.org NOTE: Havening Touch Technique also works well in conjunction with Affirmations. When you couple a physical action with a mental thought process the positive messages to the brain are reinforced.
Reiki	If you are attracted to this healing model, look for Reiki courses and therapists online. www.reiki.org.uk www.healing-reiki.org.uk
Healing Counselling & Standard Medicine	There are many forms of healing, counselling and therapy available with kind and supportive therapists. Your medical doctor can also assist with counselling and/or medication if you wish to compliment the above with a more conventional approach.

'You practice FORGIVENESS to let others know that you no longer wish to be in a state of hostility with them and to free yourself from the self-defeating energy of resentment'. Dr Wayne Dyer.

NOTES

LONELINESS

LONELINESS

Loneliness can be felt within relationships. But it takes on a depth and intensity after a relationship has ended, when you can experience such sadness and sorrow. It can also have a physical effect when you reach for comfort in food or alcohol and don't want to go outside for a walk or exercise.

Feelings of loneliness and isolation can cause us to lock down the heart and retreat as a defensive mechanism to protect from being hurt again. We sometimes hang onto this feeling of isolation, even wallow, as a sort of comfort, and can feel a victim of life.

For us to heal, it is important that we find ways to let go and move on from these feelings so that we can open our hearts again and let in love and friendship.

Use whichever of the Healing Companions you resonate with, however I would guide you to look at the sections on Natural Essences and Essential Oils as these remedies are very helpful in quickly changing how you feel. They also help in releasing difficult emotions so that you can feel more peaceful and contented.

HEALING COMPANIONS - LONELINESS

Physical Exercise	Pets can offer companionship and comfort at this time. Borrow one if you don't have a pet of your own. Volunteer at an animal sanctuary or offer to walk a neighbour's dog. Hug a teddy bear.
Music	You may want to express your sadness and listen to songs about loneliness. While it's good to release your feelings, also look for music to lift your spirits Search YouTube for 'uplifting music.
Inspired Reading	'The Anatomy of Loneliness' - Teal Swan 'Eleanor Oliphant is Completely Fine' - Gail Honeyman 'The Deeper Wound: Recovering the Soul from Fear and Suffering' - Deepak Chopra
Meditation	If you are suffering with loneliness, have the intention to befriend yourself. You can ask for spiritual comfort from the divine in whatever form you perceive them (God/Goddess/Divine Spirit/Angels). They can comfort you with their presence, helping you to heal and feel more peaceful. *Invite the divine in with a meditation on the heart. Feel your heart as a soft, warm enclosure; settle there with your attention, and rest as long as you wish. If you repeat this technique enough times, you will find that the presence of spirit becomes very real and accessible *Adapted from ''The Deeper Wound: Recovering the Soul from Fear and Suffering' – Deepak Chopra www.yogajournal.com/meditation/deepak-chopras-7-step-meditation-to-open-your-heart www.wikihow.com/Overcome-Loneliness-Through-Meditation-and-Positive-Thinking

Affirm	'Loneliness isn't a final destination'*
	'My future is filled with laughter, good times and there are beautiful memories to be made' thecoffeybreak.com/blog-2/2018/4/10/16-affirmations-to-combat-feelings-of-loneliness
	'I will open my heart and allow others into my life'- Louise L Hay
	'I deserve a beautiful & happy life' - Louise L Hay
	More affirmations at:
	www.louisehay.com/affirmations
	Affirmations also work well in conjunction with Havening Touch Technique. When you couple a physical action with a mental thought process, the positive messages to the brain are reinforced.
Essential Oils	Rose - is deeply nurturing and comforting and supports letting go of barriers around the heart.
	Melissa - increases joy and optimism and helps to let go of despair.
	Cedarwood - inspires feelings of belonging and helps the heart open to receive love and support from others.
	Wild Orange - is joyful and uplifting
	Oil Blends: 'Align' from Do Terra
	www.tisserand.com/essential-oils
	www.quinessence.com
	www.nealsyardremedies.com
	www.doterra.com/GB/en_GB

Natural Remedies & Essences	'Awakening the Heart' from Crystal Herbs www.crystalherbs.com/selfhelp/lonelines.asp BACH FLOWER REMEDIES Honeysuckle - for living in memories Willow - when feeling resentful or that life is unfair Heather - if you are finding it difficult being alone. www.bachflower.com/original-bach-flower-remedies www.rosetodd.com/bach-flower-essences
Crystals	Rose Quartz - the stone of unconditional love. It radiates gentle, soothing vibrations that regulate your emotions and restore your emotional nature after overwhelming events. Rhodochrosite - teaches the heart how to assimilate painful feelings without shutting down. It releases resentment and helps you to let go. www.crystalguidance.com/crystaltip/loneliness. Judy Hall is the pioneer of Crystal Healing, more information can be found at: judyhall.co.uk
Havening Touch	If you are attracted to this self-healing method you can find more details online and at www.havening.org NOTE: Havening Touch Technique also works well in conjunction with Affirmations. When you couple a physical action with a mental thought process the positive messages to the brain are reinforced.

Reiki	If you are attracted to this healing model, look for Reiki courses and therapists online. www.reiki.org.uk www.healing-reiki.org.uk
EFT Emotional Freedom Technique	If you are attracted to this healing model you can find more details at www.thetappingsolution.com
Healing, Counselling and Standard Medicine	There are many forms of healing, counselling and therapy available with kind and supportive therapists. Your medical doctor can also assist with counselling and/or medication if you wish to compliment the above with a more conventional approach.

LOOKING FORWARD

LOOKING FORWARD

So, you have come a long way on your healing journey and are now feeling like stepping out and experiencing what the world has to offer you.

You have successfully negotiated one of the most difficult times that can be experienced by anyone. You will feel the fear of being hurt again but do what feels comfortable and only a little scary. You now have new knowledge about yourself and you know how to nurture yourself to get through difficult times. You love yourself more and are now able to love another person. This is a NEW YOU going out into the world. To reinforce this feeling, you may want a new hairstyle, lipstick, some new 'dating clothes' to enhance the courageous and loving human being you are.

Don't worry if things don't work out as you would like them at first. Every step you take is a step further down the road to your hearts' desire.

If you find yourself 'stuck' and can't move forward, (perhaps you find it difficult to be intimate with someone even though you like them, or a friend has let you down) just keep on nurturing yourself, use essential oils and natural remedies to keep your courage and spirits high. Keep saying your affirmations, talk to a counsellor or trusted friend and know that you are doing fine and that everything happens ....

'At the right time, in the right place, with the right people' -

Dr Wayne Dyer

HEALING COMPANIONS - LOOKING FORWARD

Physical Exercise	Whatever makes you feel confident and beautiful, for example - massage, facial, new hair style, getting your nails done.
	Run, dance go to the gym
Music	'All you need is Love' - John Lennon
Inspired Reading	'How to Attract your next Partner' – David Estoe, Petaltone Essences.
	www.petaltone.co.uk/products/books-products
Meditation	Look online for guided meditations - 'meditations for looking forward'.
	www.mindful.org/how-to-meditate/
Affirm	'My spirit is youthful; my outlook is always vibrant' - You can Heal your Heart by Louise L Hay & David Kessler
	'I now deserve love, romance and joy - and all the good that life has to offer me' - Louise L Hay
	'What I desire is on its way to me' - Louise L Hay
	Affirmations also work well in conjunction with Havening Touch Technique. When you couple a physical action with a mental thought process, the positive messages to the brain are reinforced.

Essential Oils	Rose - is deeply nurturing and comforting and supports letting go of barriers around the heart.
	Thyme - for moving forward and opening the heart to joy
	Cassia - for courage
	Lime - for zest for life
	Blends: 'Align' and 'Whisper' from DoTerra,
	'Release your Fears' from 'I am Fabulous - Blends for emotional well-being' - Desiree Mangandog
	www.tisserand.com/essential-oils
	www.quinessence.com
	www.nealsyardremedies.com
	www.doterra.com/GB/en_GB
Natural Remedies & Essences	BACH FLOWER REMEDIES
	Impatiens - for patience
	Wild Rose - if you lack motivation
	Larch - for confidence
	www.bachflower.com/original-bach-flower-remedies
	www.rosetodd.com/bach-flower-essences/
	PETALTONE REMEDIES
	Tantric Love Essences for Singles
	www.petaltone.co.uk/products/essences
Crystals	Rose Quartz - attracts harmonious, long-term relationships by opening your heart chakra, allowing you to be a vision of love and beauty.

Crystals (continued)	Sunstone - brings blessings, protection, and personal power to rejuvenate your motivation. www.energymuse.com/blog/crystals-for-confidence/
Havening Touch	If you are attracted to this self-healing method you can find more details online and at www.havening.org NOTE: Havening Touch Technique also works well in conjunction with Affirmations. When you couple a physical action with a mental thought process the positive messages to the brain are reinforced.
Reiki	If you are attracted to this healing model, look for Reiki courses and therapists online. www.reiki.org.uk www.healing-reiki.org.uk
EFT Emotional Freedom Technique	If you are attracted to this healing model you can find more details at www.thetappingsolution.com
Visualisation	Draw a picture of what you would like your life to look like. Get clear on what you want in a partner and what is a definite 'no go' for you. Write these down and look at them often to keep in your mind. Sign up to online dating sites – even if you are not sure this is right for you. The function of signing up is sending a message to your subconscious/the universe that you are ready for a new relationship. Be open to any opportunities that are offered to you, you don't have to do them all, but do consider them.
"Imagine" Course	Come on my 'Imagine your Best Life' course and create a vision board for your new life. Go to www.spiritedwoman.co.uk for more details.

NOTES

A NOTE ABOUT SETBACKS

A NOTE ABOUT SETBACKS

There will probably be setbacks. You might well work through lots of feelings and start to feel better only for something to suddenly remind you of what you have lost. A song, a look, a taste or even a phone call. This is a normal part of the process, just testing you to see where you are. It does not mean you are back at the beginning of this journey, although for a time it can feel like that.

Be kind to yourself when this happens. It can be years after the breakup, time is not important. Don't beat yourself up thinking 'what is the matter with me, we broke up .... ago, why am I not over this?' Just be nurturing and supportive to yourself as you would be to a good friend finding themselves in the same position.

I advise you to look up the relevant section in this workbook and just use the remedy, oil, affirmation, book etc recommended for the stage you feel you are in. You will then start to feel better and be able to carry on with the journey where you left off.

Setbacks are also giving you a pause, time to review where you are going, and maybe you just need some space, or maybe it's another direction you need to be looking in.

GRATITUDE

GRATITUDE

Gratitude is a really powerful method of increasing happiness and one of the best ways to move forward. Finding things to be grateful for can be hard if you are suffering with difficult feelings following a loss – but it's immensely helpful. Count your blessings. Just look for one thing to be grateful for, and then the list can grow in time, write them down and look at them often.

Here are some examples to help you get started.

1. The sun is shining
2. I am warm and cosy
3. I have lovely friends/family/home/bed...
4. I have a job, or
5. I have an opportunity for a new career
6. I have flowers
7. I bask in a scented candlelit bath
8. I enjoy some real coffee and read the papers in peace
9. I cuddle my teddy/dog/cat
10. I had breakfast in bed this morning with the radio

Try also to be grateful for the good times you shared with your ex and wish them well. It can take some time to get to this point, however when you do you will realise that by refusing to shut your heart down and bravely facing the hurt and fear, you know that you are healing and moving on.

Remember Happiness is a Choice ...

Some helpful affirmations from Louise L Hay are:
1. 'I accept and love myself, exactly as I am now'
2. 'I live in the totality of possibilities'
3. 'There is always another way, I am safe'
4. 'I release, I relax and I let go'
5. 'Thank you, Thank you, Thank you'

AND NEXT

AND NEXT

When you are at the end of this journey, it is the beginning of a new road and a happier part of your life.

I hope you now feel more loving towards yourself, confident that you can easily navigate the twists and turns of your life.

If life again becomes difficult, you can always turn to the things we have discovered together on this journey. They will help you find comfort and strength and a way to move forward in a kind and gentle way.

I would love to know what parts of the workbook you liked or found particularly helpful. If you would like to form a group with others who have found this workbook helpful, or you would like some one-to-one support from me, please let me know via www.spiritedwoman.co.uk

I wish you love and happiness as you go forward

Marion

MORE READING & WEB SITES

MORE READING & WEB SITES

'You can Heal your Life'; 'Love your Body'; 'Heal your Body' and more by Louise L Hay including affirmation cards and videos.

'The Power of Intention'; 'Unstoppable Me'; The Power of Awakening'; 'The Law of Attraction' and more by Dr Wayne Dyer including YouTube videos.

'The Secret' – Rhonda Byrne

'When Everything Changes – Change Everything' and 'The Essential Path' -Neale Donald Walsch

'Jonathan Livingstone Seagull' – Richard Bach

'Seven Spiritual Laws of Success', 'The Book of Secrets'; 'You are the Universe' - Deepak Chopra

'A Course in Miracles' – Dr Helen Schucman

'The Heroes Journey' - Joseph Campbell

'Return to Love' - Marianne Williamson

'The Prophet' – Kalhil Gibran

'Sacred Poetry' - Rumi

Flourishing Goddess - feminine coach - YouTube meditations and group - flourishinggoddess.com

Melanie Beckler - www.askangels.com

Louise Carron-Harris - Medicine Woman and Reiki Master louisecarronharris.com

Jackie Singer – Shamanka, storyteller, sound healer www.thehummingbirdlodge.com

9 781782 228486